Donal Neary SJ

GW01090678

An Advent Journey

the columba press

First published in 1996 by **the columba press**
55A Spruce Avenue, Stillorgan Industrial Park, Blackrock, Co Dublin

Cover by Bill Bolger
Origination by The
Columba Press
Printed in Ireland by
Paceprint Ltd, Dublin
ISBN 1 85607 178 2
Copyright © 1996, Donal
Neary SJ

Acknowledgements:
Gill and Macmillan for
Anne Thurston, *Because of
her Testimony* and for
Donal Dorr, *Divine
Energy.* Darton, Longman
and Todd for Henri
Nouwen, *Show Me the
Way.* Paulist Press for Peter
van Bremen, *Let All God's
Glory Through.* Macmillan
Ltd for quotes from
Tagore. Ave Maria Press
for Joyce Rupp, *Praying
Our Goodbyes.* Hodder
and Stoughton for Ronald
Rolheiser, *Against an
Infinite Horizon.*
Spirituality Vol 1, No 1 for
Donough O'Shea OP,
Gaps and Glimpses. Other
reflections by the author.
A. P. Watt for The Grail
Psalms. Scripture quota-
tions from NRSV, ©
1983, 1989, Division of
Christian Education of the
National Council of the
Churches of Christ in
USA. Used by permission.
All rights reserved.

Contents

Introduction   5

Week 1   Thanks
Day 1   Waiting in Thanks   7
Day 2   Receive with Thanks   8
Day 3   I Thank you, Father   9
Day 4   Thanks and Openness   10
Day 5   Notice with Thanks   11
Day 6   Thanks for the Future   12

Week 2   Openness
Day 1   To Surprise   13
Day 2   To Love   14
Day 3   To Conversion   15
Day 4   To Forgiveness   16
Day 5   To New Life   17
Day 6   A New Way of Thinking   18

Week 3   Gifts
Day 1   Of Praise   19
Day 2   Of Light   20
Day 3   Of Fullness   21
Day 4   Of Life   22
Day 5   Of Jesus   23
Day 6   Of Mary   24

Week 4   Yearnings
Day 1   For the Kingdom   25
Day 2   For Justice   26
Day 3   For Good Things for Others   27
Day 4   For Hope   28
Day 5   For Heaven   29
Day 6   Mixed up Yearnings   30

Introduction

An Advent Journey invites you to journey towards Christmas with thanks, openness, awareness and yearning. The thoughts and words of the Scripture may help you find God in these central experiences of life, for we are most ourselves when we are grateful, open, yearning and allowing ourselves be moved towards conversion to God in Jesus Christ.[1]

'Gratefulness,' writes Peter van Bremen, 'creates a positive attitude towards life and opens a joyful way to finding God in everything.'[2] The first week is to be touched by the gratitude which we feel in the light of God. In the second week we allow ourselves be challenged to conversion, and then in the third week to be aware of the gifts of God in life. The fourth week opens us to pray within some of the deeper yearnings of our hearts.

How to pray with this book
This book may be used personally each day or may also be used by a parish or other group. For the seventh day of each week, return to the day in that week which most attracted you. If a group meets for a weekly sharing on prayer, some sharing of varied insights, or help people got from the prayer-material for a week, is best. Groups who meet to share in this way might begin their meeting with the prayer-material for the day. Or it may be used in a parish or community, with music, as a simple morning or evening Advent prayer.

Praying Personally

Select a time and a place for your prayer, where you can be quiet, without interruption.

Slowly read the material for each day, reading the Scripture aloud if that suits you.

Pause when you want to, when a phrase or idea strikes you; no need to read all the material for a day if you don't wish. Stay with a word or phrase that engages you – giving you some peace, comfort, or a sense of harmony within yourself.

If you wish, talk to Jesus in your own words from the Scripture or the reflection, thanking him, asking him for what you need, or praying for someone; or simply remain silent in the presence of the Lord.

Prayer is you speaking from the heart to God, and God speaking from the heart to you.

End your prayer with some of the words of the Psalm or any prayer you like yourself.

1. You may recognise the themes of the Journey as rooted in some insights of St Ignatius of Loyola on our relationship with God. 'Finding God in all things' – an aim of St Ignatius in the spiritual life, means finding God in the gratitude and yearnings, the challenges and changes of life; it means seeing all of our lives as a gift and that the very relationship we have with God is his gift to us.

2. Peter van Bremen, *Let God's Glory Through*, c. 25, for some excellent insights on gratitude.

Introduction

We await the coming of Christ anew, again, not for the first time. Our thanks for the coming of Jesus into our lives is a beginning of new openness, new hope and new conversion. We give thanks, from the depths of our hearts, for the ways God has graced our lives.

Scripture Reading

(Lk 1:46-47, 49)
Let the words of Mary open our souls to the mystery of gratitude in our lives.

And Mary said, My soul magnifies the Lord, and my spirit rejoices in God, my Saviour. For the Mighty One has done great things for me, and holy is his name.

Reflection

To be a saint is to be motivated by gratitude. Scripture makes this point. For example the sin of Adam and Eve was a failure in receptivity and gratitude. God gives them life, each other and the garden, and only asks them to receive it properly, in gratitude, to receive and give thanks. The original sin was precisely their refusal to do this. Instead they took the apple ... taking as by right what could only be received gratefully as gift.
[Ronald Rolheiser OMI, *Against an Infinite Horizon*]

Psalm *Psalm 15*

Lord, my heart rejoices, my soul is glad;
even my body shall rest in safety.
For you will not leave my soul among the dead,
nor let your beloved know decay.

You will show me the path of life,
the fullness of joy in your presence,
at your right hand happiness forever.

Introduction

Being grateful for the love of God in our lives gives an openness so that all of life can be received with thanks; even what seems painful now may be received in the trust that God is in all that we experience.

Scripture Reading

(Lk 2:19)

During all Jesus' life, especially in times that tested her faith, Mary would relive with thanks and awe the visit of the shepherds.

But Mary treasured all these words and pondered them in her heart.

Reflection

Memory is a storehouse of grace … always accessible to you … not just a 'recalling' memory, but the memory that relives. And the feelings return, and the gratitude. The sunshine within the rain. The chapters of the book of the heart are written with the love we meet and experience, the love we watch and receive, and most of all in the love we give. Love stays alive in the memory of the heart. Nothing can take it away, for it is lasting. Love touched close at hand never dies. Love that was heard in silent presence or tasted in shared laughter, embrace or struggle, lives on … the fountain inside, dancing and welling up to what we name as eternity. Love felt in shared sympathy and care given over a long time leaves its own echo in the memory of the heart. For compassion and sympathy leave their footprints on life. Be grateful for what is imprinted of love and of God in the memory.

Psalm *Psalm 85*

I will praise you, Lord, with all my heart
and glorify your name forever;
for your love to me has been great;
you have saved me from the depths of the grave.

Week 1 Day 3:   I Thank you, Father

Introduction

Jesus was a man of thankful heart, who saw within all around him the graces and the goodness of God; who always noticed the care of God for the poor and in bad times.

Scripture Reading

(Mt 11:25-26)

Jesus' prayer sums up an attitude he had always – of gratitude to his Father for his relationship with him and his mission.

At that time Jesus said, 'I thank you, Father, Lord of heaven and earth, because you have hidden these things from the wise and the intelligent and have revealed them to infants; yes, Father, for such was your gracious will.'

Reflection

It is no coincidence that when giving us the Eucharist, Christ said, 'Receive and give thanks'. Only after doing this do we go on to 'break and share'. Before all else, we first give thanks. To receive in gratitude is the most primary of all religious attitudes. Proper gratitude is the ultimate virtue. Holy people are people who are grateful, people who see and receive everything as gift. The converse is also true. Anyone who takes life and love for granted should not ever be confused with a saint.
[Ronald Rolheiser OMI, *Against An Infinite Horizon*]

Psalm *Psalm 103*

Bless the Lord, my soul,
my God, how great you are,
clothed in majesty and glory,
wrapped in light as in a robe.

I will sing to the Lord all my life,
make music to my God while I live.
May my thoughts be pleasing to him.
I find my joy in the Lord.

Week 1 Day 4: Thanks and Openness

Introduction

A grateful person is open to being surprised by the new, to being consoled in pain, and open to the sure hope that all emptiness will be filled.

Scripture Reading

(Lk 2:30-32)

All his life Simeon had waited for the Saviour. An emptiness never barren, always hopeful; never satisfied but in the waiting was the gift.

For my eyes have seen your salvation which you have prepared in the presence of all peoples, a light for revelation to the Gentiles and for glory to your people Israel.

Reflection

A small, wooden flute, an empty, hollow reed, rests in her silent hand.
It awaits the breath of one who creates song through its open form.
My often empty life rests in the hand of God, like the hollowed flute, it yearns for the melody which only Breath can give.
The small wooden flute and I, we need the one who breathes, we await the one who makes melody.
And the one whose touch creates, awaits our empty, ordinary forms, so that the song-starved world may be fed with golden melodies.
[Joyce Rupp]

Psalm *Psalm 117*

I will thank you for you have given answer and you are my saviour.
The stone which the builder rejected has become the corner stone.
This is the work of the Lord, a marvel in our eyes.
This day was made by the Lord, we rejoice and are glad.

Week 1 Day 5: Notice with Thanks

Introduction

Life can pass us by: simple gifts of nature and love we miss; we may also miss simple promises of love from God in his word and through others.

Scripture Reading

(Lk 2:38)

Simeon and Anna noticed that the Lord had come; others would have passed by.

At that moment she came, and began to praise God and to speak about the child to all who were looking for the redemption of Jerusalem.

Reflection

Yet sometimes when the sun comes through a gap
These men know God the Father in a tree:
The Holy Spirit is the rising sap
And Christ will be the green leaves that will come
At Easter from the sealed and guarded tomb.
                              Patrick Kavanagh.

A gap in what? A gap in the usual arrangements ... in the polished surface of routine, between carefully fitted thoughts. And he means a narrow gap, I think. Elsewhere he wrote, 'through a chink too wide there comes in no wonder'. Through a gap ... when the defences are in ruins. Through the gap in the plans to build one's life into a sealed and guarded tomb ... God grant us the uncommon gift of allowing gaps; through them can burst the surprise of Easter-faith. The sun shines briefly through and we have no claim on it, nor purchase; it is an unaccountable gift. Many have reprimanded us about the 'god of the gaps': when we want God to fill the gaps in our lives. God, we know, doesn't fill gaps; on the contrary. God shines through them.
[Donogh O'Shea in 'Gaps and Glimpses', *Spirituality, 1*]

Psalm *Psalm 106*

Let them thank the Lord for his love,
the wonders he does for his people.
Let them exalt him in the gathering of the people,
and praise him in the meeting of the elders.
He raises the needy from distress,
the upright see it and rejoice.
Whoever is wise, heed these things
and consider the love of the Lord.

Week 1 Day 6:   Thanks for the Future

Introduction
Give thanks before the future happens – that is the mark of the one who trusts. This is thanks for the guiding hand of God in our lives, as it was for Mary and Joseph before the birth of Christ.

Scripture Reading
(Mt 2:13-14)
Now after they had left, an angel of the Lord appeared to Joseph in a dream and said, 'Get up, take the child and his mother, and flee to Egypt, and remain there until I tell you; for Herod is about to search for the child, to destroy him.' Then Joseph got up, took the child and his mother by night, and went to Egypt.

Reflection
God's love is such a powerful companion for us that no matter how searing or how intense the hurt of a loss is we know that our spirit need not be destroyed by it; we know that God will help us to recover our hope, our courage and our direction in life ... Love endures and goes on, in spite of all the feelings of grief inside us. Deep down we know that love can go with us beyond death. People who say that they won't love again, won't trust again, won't risk again, won't try again, are in the stage the disciples were in when they were overcome with the death of Jesus and walked dejected and downhearted, thinking their lives would never hold meaning and happiness again. The human spirit is astounding in its resiliency and its ability to recover hope. This is what the resurrection proclaims: the possibility of transformation, the belief that we can be filled with new life, that the future will bless us.
[Joyce Rupp, *Praying Our Goodbyes*]

Psalm *From 1 Sam 2*
Into your hands, O Lord, I commend my spirit.
Lord, it is you who give life and death,
who bring us to the grave and back;
it is you who give poverty and riches,
you bring us low and raise us on high.

Week 2 Day 1:   Openness to Surprise

Introduction
God is ever-new, as is seen in the birth of Jesus. Can you be surprised by God?

Scripture Reading
(Lk 1:31, 33-35)
'And now, you will conceive in your womb and bear a son, and you will name him Jesus … He will reign over the house of Jacob forever, and of his kingdom there will be no end.' Mary said to the angel, 'How can this be, since I am a virgin?' The angel said to her, 'The Holy Spirit will come upon you, and the power of the Most High will over-shadow you; there-fore the child to be born will be holy; he will be called Son of God.'

Reflection
Now I know it is not I who pray but the Spirit of God who prays in me. Indeed when God's glory dwells in me, there is nothing too far away, nothing too painful, nothing too strange or too familiar that it cannot contain and renew by its touch. Every time I recognise the glory of God in me and give it space to manifest itself to me, all that is human can be brought there and nothing will be the same again. Once in a while I just know it. Of course God hears my prayer, he himself prays in me and touches the whole world with his love right here and now.
[Henri Nouwen, *Show Me the Way*]

Psalm *Psalm 8*
How great is your name, O Lord our God,
through all the earth.
You have made us little less than gods,
with glory and honour you crowned us,
gave us power over the works of your hand,
put all things under our feet.

Week 2 Day 2:   Openness to Love

Introduction

We are made for love; and we yearn for love that is total. Fears can block our openness to love; the love of God is always in our reach. God loves us of himself and through others.

Scripture Reading

(Jn 3:16)

The love of God is total, and is the reason for the birth of Jesus among us.

'For God so loved the world that he gave his only Son, so that everyone who believes in him may not perish but may have eternal life.'

Reflection

When one falls in love, life becomes suffused with new colour, new life, new energy and new hope. All this is experienced as an unexpected and unmerited gift. Some are content to revel in the gift, aware now that life is far richer and deeper than they had realised. Others experience the Giver in the gift; they sense that what they have been given is a share in a divine love which can permeate and renew this broken world.

[Donal Dorr, *Divine Energy*]

Psalm *Psalm 18*

I love you, Lord, my strength,
my rock, my fortress, my saviour.
My God is the rock where I take refuge,
my shield, my mighty help, my stronghold.
The Lord is worthy of all praise.

Week 2 Day 3:   Openness to Conversion

Introduction

The coming of Jesus into the world was unexpected: he was born poor, lowly, unheralded by pomp. Those who reflected on this birth were challenged to a conversion of mind and heart.

Scripture Reading

(Mt 1:20)

All involved in the birth of Christ found big changes in their lives – see this in the life of Joseph.

But just when he had resolved to do this, an angel of the Lord appeared to him in a dream and said, 'Joseph, son of David, do not be afraid to take Mary as your wife, for the child conceived in her is from the Holy Spirit.'

Reflection

The converted person does not say that nothing matters any more, but that everything that *is* happens in God and that he is the dwelling place where we come to know the true order of things. Instead of saying: 'Nothing matters any more, since I know that God exists,' the converted person says: 'All is now clothed in divine light and therefore nothing can be unimportant ...' The converted person sees, hears and understands with a divine eye, a divine ear, a divine heart. The converted person knows himself or herself and all the world in God. The converted person is where God is, and from that place everything matters: giving water, clothing the naked, working for a new world order, saying a prayer, smiling at a child, reading a book, and sleeping in peace. All has become different while all remains the same.

[Henri Nouwen, *Show Me the Way*]

Psalm *Psalm 85*

Teach me, Lord, your ways,
that I may not stray from your loyalty;
let my heart's one aim be to love your name.

I thank you, Lord, with all my heart,
I will glorify your name for ever,
for your faithful love to me is so great
that you have raised me from the depths of the grave.

Introduction

Love founded in God is ready to forgive, even before the other looks for it. This is the love of God.

Scripture Reading

(Lk 1:68, 77-79)
This birth-hymn for John the Baptist praises God for the forgiveness of sins.

Blessed be the Lord God of Israel,
for he has looked favourably on his people and redeemed them ... To give knowledge of salvation to his people by the forgiveness of their sins. By the tender mercy of our God, the dawn from on high will break upon us ...

Reflection

Even the *awareness* of guilt hinges on the inner certainty that one is truly loved, even with one's guilt. Only people who know they are completely and fully loved, can experience full-fledged guilt. After all, guilt is precisely the abuse of this love. But it is only when we believe, or at least have a hunch, that this love is greater than our guilt could ever be, that we can courageously face it ... We live steadily on forgiveness. When it is omitted for any length of time, we become ill in the same way as when certain vitamins are lacking for too long. To live on forgiveness is a vital Christian art. Whoever has mastered this art finds forgiveness continuously and in many different forms ... Forgiveness has to be both given and received. We cannot produce it ourselves.
[Peter van Bremen, *Let All God's Glory Through*]

Psalm *Psalm 99*

Indeed how good is the Lord,
eternal his merciful love,
he is faithful from age to age.

Week 2 Day 5:   Openness to New Life

Introduction

Mary and Elizabeth rejoiced in the new life which they felt inside them. All new life, physical or spiritual, emotional or relational, is a sharing in the life of God.

Scripture Reading
(Lk 1:43-44)
A cry of joy for new life when Mary met Elizabeth.

'And why has this happened to me, that the mother of my Lord comes to me? For as soon as I heard the sound of your greeting, the child in my womb leaped for joy.'

Reflection

Knowing what it means to bring forth life, we will be unwilling to destroy life ... Stories about birth, which are now exceptional and marginal, made up a large part of the stories which formed us. The Hebrew Scriptures are full of stories about birth to people who imagined they were self-sufficient. They recognised the breath of life as God's gift, and celebrated the fragile wonder of new life.
[Anne Thurstson, *Because of her Testimony*]

Psalm   *Psalm 41*

Like the deer that yearns
for running streams,
so my soul is yearning
for you, my God.

My soul is thirsting for God,
the God of my life;
when can I enter and see
the face of God?

Week 2 Day 6:   A New Way of Thinking

Introduction
Jesus turns social prejudice upside down in the place of his birth, the stable of a poor inn.

Scripture Reading
(Lk 2:6-7)
Notice the simplicity of the birth of the Son of God.

While they were there, the time came for her to deliver her child. And she gave birth to her firstborn son and wrapped him in bands of cloth, and laid him in a manger, because there was no place for them in the inn.

Reflection
Most surprising of all though is the story of the woman at the well. This is a truly scandalous meeting on two levels: firstly because Jesus is speaking to a Samaritan and, as the text tells us, 'Jews have no dealings with Samaritans'; and secondly, because Jesus speaks to a woman and is prepared to drink from her jar. This is probably the most extraordinary aspect, that Jesus makes a request, establishes a basis of equality and indicates to the astonished woman that he treats her with a respect which is clearly not traditionally accorded to Samaritans or to women. The woman knows that both her race and her sex disqualify her and yet Jesus speaks to her and asks her for water.
[Anne Thurston, *Because of her Testimony*]

Psalm *Psalm 4*
'What can bring us happiness?' many say.
Let the light of your face shine on us, O Lord.
You have put into my heart a greater joy
than they have from an abundance of corn and new wine.
I will lie down and sleep comes at once,
for you alone, Lord, make me dwell in safety.

Week 3 Day 1:   Gift of Praise

Introduction

The coming of the Lord invoked praise in all who met Jesus: praise for the end of the waiting, praise for the fulfilment of the promise. The beginning of praising God is itself a gift from God.

Scripture Reading

(Lk 1:68, 79)
Blessed be the Lord God of Israel!
for he has looked favourably on his people and redeemed them.
To give light to those who sit in darkness and in the shadow of death,
to guide our feet into the way of peace.

Reflection

God is more present than many imagine. The abandonment, the total solitude of Christ on the cross, has yielded its fruit. It seemed as though our eyes could see only what is negative. But the power of the one crucified has set the earth on fire, and the Spirit is doing his work in each person's heart. We must cleanse our sleepy eyes and learn how to see. We shall be surprised, and we shall burst into an irrepressible shout of praise.
[Pedro Arrupe SJ]

Psalm *Psalm 112*

Praise, O servants of the Lord,
praise the name of the Lord!
May the name of the Lord be praised
both now and for evermore.
From the rising of the sun to its setting,
praised be the name of the Lord!

Week 3 Day 2: Gift of Light

Introduction

Light is a well-loved symbol for Christmas – candles, the lights on a tree, the name of Jesus, 'light of the world'.

Scripture Reading

(Jn 1:4-5, 9)
What has come into being in him was life, and the life was the light of all people. The light shines in the darkness, and the darkness did not overcome it. The true light, which enlightens everyone, was coming into the world.

Reflection

God will enter into your night, as the ray of the sun enters into the dark, hard earth, driving right down to the roots of the tree, and there, unseen, unknown, unfelt in the darkness, filling the tree with life, a sap of fire will suddenly break out, high above that darkness, into living leaf and flame.
[Caryll Houselander]

Psalm *Psalm 27*

The Lord is my light and my help,
whom shall I fear?
The Lord is the stronghold of my life,
Of whom shall I be afraid?

Week 3 Day 3:   Gift of Fullness

Introduction

In the emptiness of life and its seeming lack of meaning can be found the fullness of God in Jesus Christ.

Scripture Reading

(Lk 1:13-15)
The promise of birth is the promise of the gift of new life, of fullness, to the emptiness of the home of Elizabeth and Zechariah.

But the angel said to him, 'Do not be afraid, Zechariah, for your prayer has been heard. Your wife Elizabeth will bear you a son and you will name him John. You will have joy and gladness, and many will rejoice at his birth, for he will be great in the sight of the Lord.'

Reflection

On that night when the storm broke open my door
I did not know that you entered my room through the ruins,
For the lamp was blown out, and it became dark;
I stretched my arms to the sky in search of help.
I lay on the dust waiting in the tumultuous dark and
I knew not that storm was your own banner.
When the morning came I saw you standing upon
the emptiness that was spread over my house.
[Tagore]

Psalm *Psalm 16*

And so my heart rejoices, my soul is glad;
even my body shall rest in safety.
You will show me the path of life,
the fullness of joy in your presence,
at your right hand happiness forever.

Week 3 Day 4:   Gift of Life

Introduction
We celebrate the birth of God on earth; in this birth the life of eternity touches the life of the earth and all are one.

Scripture Reading
(Jn 1:3)
Jesus lived in the fullness of the life of all creation.

All things came into being through him, and without him not one thing came into being.

Reflection
The same stream of life that runs through my veins night and day runs through the world and dances in rhythmic measures.
It is the same life that shoots in joy through the dust of the earth in numberless blades of grass and breaks into tumultuous waves of leaves and flowers.
It is the same life that is rocked in the ocean-cradle of birth and of death, in ebb and in flow.
I feel my limbs are made glorious by the touch of this world of life. And my pride is from the life-throb of ages dancing in my blood this moment.
[Tagore]

Psalm *Psalm 34*
Come, my children, listen to me,
I will teach you the fear of the Lord.
Who among you delights in life,
Longs for time to enjoy prosperity?

Guard your tongue from evil,
your lips from any breath of deceit.
Turn away from evil and do good,
seek peace and pursue it.

Week 3 Day 5: Gift of Jesus

Introduction

We pray to know Jesus as the gift of God. Every child, like Jesus, is a gift of life and from God.

Scripture Reading

(Jn 1:14)
And the Word became flesh and lived among us, and we have seen his glory, the glory as of a father's only son, full of grace and truth.

Reflection

'The gift of a child' is often how a birth is announced. For Mary and Joseph it was the same. Jesus was a gift of God to them, a gift awaited and expected by many. It was a mysterious gift, for Jesus is the mystery of God made flesh among us. The gift of God's love and forgiveness to the world has come through these two people of faith. The gift of God to people then is the same gift of God to us now. Because of Jesus we know that God is close, compassionate, caring and concerned for our needs. We know God has a special eye for those in trouble and those who are poor. We know too, like Mary, he would be sent for the 'rise and fall of many' – the gift of Jesus is a 'tough gift' at times, calling us to stand in love for the concerns he died for. The love of God and the challenges of God, coming through Jesus, are life-giving foundations for the love and decisions of our lives. For this gift we are grateful.

Psalm *Psalm 97*
All the ends of the earth have seen
the salvation of our God.
Shout to the Lord all the earth,
ring out your joy.

Week 3 Day 6:   Gift of Mary

Introduction
At the cross Mary was 'given' to us as a mother from God. She was this to Jesus all during his life, and thus is our mother from the moment of her vocation to be the mother of God. She knew the pains and joys of being a mother.

Scripture Reading
(Lk 1:48-49)
Mary's role is to last forever.
Surely, from now on all generations will call me blessed; for the Mighty One has done great things for me, and holy is his name.

Reflection
Women attempting to articulate the experience of birth cannot relate to the birthing mother Mary, who seems to have been removed from the pain of childbirth and the total physical involvement entailed in giving birth. In suggesting that Mary bypasses this physical process, are we not diminishing rather than increasing her holiness? Are we not also diminishing the power of the Incarnation? To obliterate the pain and tears at the beginning of the life of Jesus seems to me to be as little justified as the fallacious belief that Jesus did not actually suffer physical pain on the cross. In both instances we are talking about pain which has a purpose, pain which is a necessary prelude to glory. Can we not imagine that Jesus suffered the pain of separation when he emerged into the world that would reject him? It is here that birth and death meet as thresholds to new life. It is here that the cry from the cross and the cry from the womb yield to life, to resurrection.
[Anne Thurston, *Because of her Testimony*]

Psalm *Psalm 130*
O Lord, my heart is not proud nor haughty my eyes.
I have not gone after things too great
nor marvels beyond me.
Truly I have set my soul in silence and peace.
As a child has rest in its mother's arms,
even so my soul.
Hope in the Lord, both now and forever.

Week 4 Day 1:   Yearning for the Kingdom

Introduction

Simeon was among those who waited with longing for the coming of God's kingdom.

Scripture Reading

(Lk 2:25-26)
Now there was a man in Jerusalem whose name was Simeon; this man was righteous and devout, looking forward to the con-solation of Israel, and the Holy Spirit rested on him. It had been revealed to him by the Holy Spirit that he would not see death before he had seen the Lord's Messiah.

Reflection

It helps now and then to step back and take the long view. The kingdom is not only beyond our efforts, it is even beyond our vision. We accomplish in our lifetime only a tiny fraction of the magnificent enterprise that is God's work ... No programme accomplishes the church's mission. No set of goals includes everything.

This is what we are about. We plant the seeds that one day will grow. We water seeds already planted, knowing that they hold future promise ... We cannot do everything and there is a sense of liberation in realising that. This enables us to do something and to do it very well ... We may never see the end results, but that is the difference between the master builder and the workers.

We are workers, not master builders, ministers, not messiahs. We are prophets of a future not our own. [Oscar Romero]

Psalm *Psalm 62*

O God, you are my God, for you I long,
for you my soul is thirsting.
My body pines for you,
like a dry, weary land without water.

Week 4 Day 2: Yearning for Justice

Introduction

We wince when we hear of others being badly treated, being deprived of dignity, when there is injustice. The Christian yearns like Jesus for justice.

Scripture Reading

(Lk 1:53)
Mary sings of the justice we long for, and from this sense of justice came Jesus' preferential love for the poor.

He has filled the hungry with good things, and sent the rich away empty.

Reflection

The mother who watches over her sick child, or who angrily defends her child, is being drawn out of herself into relationships with another. Can we extend the boundaries of that care from the bodily connection between parent and child to a concern for all the weak and vulnerable? What we find imperfectly in the love of human mothers, we find perfectly in the love of God. The love of God is totally inclusive, calling us to a love for one another which resists distinctions made on the grounds of race and sex ... 'Mothering' becomes a metaphor for solidarity with the vulnerable which knows no familial or gender boundaries.
[Anne Thurston, *Because of her Testimony*]

Psalm *Psalm 85*

Lord, may faithful love and loyalty join together,
saving justice and peace embrace.
May loyalty spring up from the earth,
and may justice lean down from heaven.

Introduction

Many of our prayers are for others. For our children, young people; for our sick and dying; for all who are dear to us. May God bless our good yearnings for them.

Scripture Reading

(Mt 1:22-23)
God wants good things for us, so he sent his son.

All this took place to fulfil what had been spoken by the Lord through the prophet: 'Look, the virgin shall conceive and bear a son, and they shall name him Emmanuel,' which means, 'God is with us.'

Reflection

The yearnings of our prayer bring us out of ourselves to want good things for others. The prayer of parents centres much on their children, of teachers on their pupils, of children for parents. As real prayer leads into real love, so real prayer leads us to want the best for others. Love is shown in our desires for the best for others, as well as our doing good for them. When we pray for others, we open ourselves to loving them for their own sakes. Prayer leads us also to desire the best for people we may dislike, or for people we have difficulties and differences with. Our Christmas prayer unites us with everyone, as we are all invited to the same Jesus in his place of birth. At our best we wish the best for others: that they may find the best in life. These good wishes are yearnings given us by God. As we pray at Christmas, let our prayers include the real yearnings we have for the happiness of others. When we pray for each other, the Holy Spirit, who prayed deeply within Mary, prays within us.

Psalm *Psalm 132*

How good and pleasant it is
when people live in unity!
It is like precious oil upon the head ...
it is like the dew of Mount Hermon which falls
on the heights of Sion.
For there the Lord gives his blessing,
life forever.

Week 4 Day 4: Yearning for Hope

Introduction

The hope we see in the birth of the Christ-child is the hope of the One who was raised from death. All human life is made hopeful by the birth of Jesus.

Scripture Reading

(Lk 1:73-74, 78)
The song of Zechariah is a song of joy and hope at the presence of the Lord.

The oath that he swore to our ancestor Abraham, to grant us that we, being rescued from the hands of our enemies, might serve him without fear ...
By the tender mercy of our God, the dawn from on high will break upon us.

Reflection

Jesus is born, as was each of us, in a woman's pain and distress. The story, so much wiser than we are, says that – even when we feel lost and abandoned – God is here, with us and within us. Medieval people without the kind of intellectual sophistication that finds a Nativity play silly ... knew in a direct way that this event was cause for tremendous rejoicing, was the sort of insight that changes lives. We too are at liberty to use the Christmas story by discovering that the meaning, the purpose, the love, the joy, the hope, is right here in the middle of our lives. Where we are most happy, or most troubled, most successful or most foolish, most proud of ourselves, or most ashamed, most secure or most anxious, most cheerful or most depressed, the divinity is already present. Like the shepherds or the wise men, we have simply to recognise that we are touched by the marvellous event.
[Monica Furlong, *Independent*, Dec 30 1995]

Psalm *Psalm 43*

In the daytime God sends his faithful love,
and even at night;
the song it inspires in me
is a prayer to my living God.

Week 4 Day 5: Yearning for Heaven

Introduction
The one we celebrate at Christmas came from heaven, to bring us back. Our yearning for full happiness, joy, peace, love and for all that lasts forever, hints at the human yearning for God and for heaven.

Scripture Reading
(Jn 1:1-3)
The One we celebrate at Christmas lives from eternity, and lives now in heaven. We will join him there.

In the beginning was the Word, and the Word was with God, and the Word was God. All things came into being through him, and without him not one thing came into being.

Reflection
Whether we recognise it or not, there is a homesick crane in each of us … The homesick crane in us knows that life is a journey, that we can never completely settle down and settle in, because 'home is the place we are always going to but never arrive'. The homesick crane in us is the pilgrim who never arrives, who is always going home, sometimes not having any idea of which way to turn but knowing deep within that there is a goal awaiting and that it is well worth the journey with all its ups and downs, with all its hellos and goodbyes.
[Joyce Rupp]

Psalm *Psalm 26*
There is one thing I ask of the Lord,
for this I long,
to live in the house of the Lord,
all the days of my life,
to savour the sweetness of the Lord,
to behold his temple.

Week 4 Day 6:   Mixed Up Yearnings

Introduction

Each of us has many desires. We make decisions and live within ambiguous desires, wanting good and the less-good at the same time.

Scripture Reading

(Mt 1:21)

Jesus saves us from sinful desires and nourishes our good desires.

She will give birth to a son and you must name him Jesus, because he is the one who is to save his people from their sins.

Reflection

In the world's dusty road I lost my heart,
but you picked it up in your hand.
I gleaned sorrow while seeking for joy,
but the sorrow which you sent to me has turned to joy in my life.
My desires were scattered in pieces,
you gathered them and strung them in your love.
And while I wandered from door to door,
every step led me to your gate.
[Tagore]

Psalm *Psalm 85*

Turn your ear O Lord and give answer,
for I am poor and needy ...
Show me, Lord, your way,
so that I may walk in your truth.
Console me and give me your help.